A World of Difference

Let's Go!

By Karin Luisa Badt

CHILDRENS PRESS®
CHICAGO

Picture Acknowledgments

Cover (top left), NASA; cover (left), © Victor Englebert; cover (top right), © Penny Tweedie/Tony Stone Images; cover (bottom right), © Robert Frerck/Odyssey/Frerck/Chicago; 1, Joyce Photographics/Valan; 3 (top), UPI/Bettmann; 3 (bottom), © Jevan Berrange/South American Pictures; 4, H. Armstrong Roberts; 5 (top), Ivy Images; 5 (bottom), © David Austen/Ivy Images; 6 (left), The Bettmann Archive; 6 (right), © Robert Frerck/Odyssey/Frerck/Chicago; 7 (top), ©Hugh Sitton/Tony Stone Images; 7 (center), 7 (bottom), © Robert Frerck/Odyssey/Frerck/Chicago; 8 (left), The Bettmann Archive; 8 (right), © Ed Pritchard/Tony Stone Images; 9 (left), © Sue Ann Miller/Tony Stone Images; 9 (top right), © Robin Smith/Tony Stone Images; 9 (bottom right), © Geisser/H. Armstrong Roberts; 10 (left), © Victor Englebert; 10 (top right), © Jeff Greenberg/PhotoEdit; 10 (bottom right), © Jevan Berrange/South American Pictures; 11 (left), © Penny Tweedie/Tony Stone Images; 11 (top left), © George Hunter/Tony Stone Images; 11 (bottom right), © Victor Englebert; 12 (top), © Wendy Stone/Odyssey/Chicago; 12 (bottom), The Bettmann Archive; 13 (left), © Porterfield/Chickering; 13 (top right), © Robert Frerck/Odyssey/Frerck/Chicago; 13 (bottom right), The Bettmann Archive; 14 (top), © Bob & Ira Spring; 14 (bottom), © Jean Higgins/Unicorn Stock Photos; 15, © Robert Frerck/Odyssey/Frerck/Chicago; 16 (top), The Bettmann Archive; 16 (bottom), © Victor Englebert; 17 (top), © Manley/SuperStock International, Inc.; 17 (center), © Porterfield/Chickering; 17 (bottom), NASA; 18 (top), © John Elk III; 18 (bottom), © Christine Osborne/Valan; 19 (top left), © Jeff Greenberg/PhotoEdit; 19 (top right), © Kirkendall/Spring; 19 (bottom), © Kennon Cooke/Valan; 20 (top), Tony Stone Images; 20 (bottom), © P. Degginger/H. Armstrong Roberts; 21 (top) NASA; 21 (bottom), © Tony Morrison/South American Pictures; 22 (top), UPI/Bettmann; 22 (bottom), Ivy Images; 23 (top), © John Elk III; 23 (bottom), The Bettmann Archive; 24 (top), © Carl Purcell; 24 (bottom), Joyce Photographics/Valan; 25 (top left), © Brian Seed/Tony Stone Images; 25 (top right), © Robert Frerck/Odyssey/Frerck/Chicago; 25 (bottom right), Photri; 26 (top), Chip and Rosa Maria de la Cueva Peterson; 26 (center), © Cheryl Sheridan/Odyssey/Chicago; 26 (bottom), © J.R. Page/Valan; 27 (top), © Victor Englebert; 27 (bottom), United Nations; 28 (left), © Aubrey Diem/Valan; 28 (right), © Cameramann International, Ltd.; 29 (top), © Jeff Greenberg/PhotoEdit; 29 (bottom), © Jeff Greenberg/Unicorn Stock Photos; 30 (left), © Victor Englebert; 30 (right), © Malak Photographs Limited/Ivy Images; 31 (top left), © Intn'l Photobank/Ivy Images; 31 (top right), © Inge Spence/Tom Stack & Associates; 31 (center right), © Robert Francis/South American Pictures; 31 (bottom), Chip and Rosa Maria de la Cueva Peterson

On the cover

Top: People riding a mule, Morocco
Bottom left: People riding a bicycle, Bolivia
Bottom right: A *jeepney,* a form of public
 transportation in the Philippines

On the title page

A public bus in New Zealand

Project Editor Shari Joffe
Design Herman Adler Design Group
Photo Research Feldman & Associates

Badt, Karin Luisa.
 Let's go! / by Karin Luisa Badt.
  p. cm. — (A World of difference)
 Includes index.
 ISBN 0-516-08195-0
 1. Transportation — Juvenile literature. [1. Transportation.]
 I. Title. II. Series.
 TA1149.B33 1995
 629.04 — dc20   94-36911
                                                        CIP
                                                        AC

Contents

A Quick Trip Through Time

Did you ever think about how important traveling is in your life? You travel to get to school, to visit your friends, to go to parties and sports events.

How do you get to where you want to go? For short distances, you may walk or ride a bicycle. For longer distances, you may ride in a car, hop on a bus, or even take an airplane.

But it hasn't always been so easy. A hundred and fifty years ago, there were no cars or buses or planes. The bicycle had been invented, but it was so bulky and awkward, it was almost as easy to carry one as to ride one! If we go back even further in time, we can *really* appreciate modern-day vehicles.

Egyptian sledge About 4,500 years ago, the Egyptians used sledges to transport huge stone blocks, some weighing 5,000 pounds, for the gigantic statues and pyramids they were building. Imagine pulling that much weight!

Ten thousand years ago, people had to walk everywhere they went. If they had something heavy to carry, they tied it onto a forked branch and dragged it behind them. It wasn't easy to move around in those days.

Still, early people had to travel. For one thing, they had to find food. For another, they often had to search for a better place to live—just like many people do today. Inventing better methods of transportation soon became a priority.

The first vehicle to be invented was the sledge, which is similar to a sled. People of ancient times used sledges

Dugout canoe, Papua New Guinea (right) In many parts of the world, people have preserved the ancient technique of making canoes from hollowed-out logs.

to pull all kinds of things around; fuel, food, even other people. Sledges could be dragged over many kinds of terrain—even over snow, grass, sand, and marsh—and so they were popular throughout the world.

Then, about 5,500 years ago, in Sumer (present-day Iraq), something fantastic happened: the wheel was invented! The wheel made it possible to roll things along rather than drag them. All you had to do was attach a couple of wheels to an axle, secure the axle underneath some boards, and you had a handy cart. Tamed animals, such as oxen, could be yoked to the cart to pull it.

Still, it wasn't easy to travel by land. The few roads that existed were poor. If you wanted to take a cart to the next village, you had to get around obstacles like trees, rocks, and prickly thornbushes. All in all, it was easier to travel by water. Rivers and streams were wonderful "roads" that nature had

Native American travois
Traditionally, Plains Indians used a vehicle called a *travois*—a net or platform attached to two poles— to transport their belongings from place to place. Originally, these were pulled by women or dogs. After about 1600, when Europeans brought horses to the Americas, horses were used instead.

already made. You could float down them without much getting in your way.

In the early days of human civilization, the only way to travel in the water was to swim—or hold onto a floating log. Eventually, people came up with the idea of traveling *inside* a log. The inside of a log could be burned out or scooped out with a sharp instrument, and then you had a boat!

The cart and the boat were very important for the development of civilization. They made it possible for people living in different places to trade goods with one another. For example, farmers used carts to transport crops from their farms to the cities.

Over the centuries, carts and boats became more sophisticated. People experimented with the cart to make it faster and more comfortable. First, the two-wheeled chariot was invented, then the four-wheeled wagon, and finally, in the 1400s, the coach. A coach is a kind of covered wagon or carriage that hangs suspended over the wheels—either by springs, or, in the early days of its invention, by leather straps. Riding in a coach was

Ancient Roman road in Turkey
Roads were very important for the development of transportation—and civilization. The ancient Romans were famous for the fine roads they built, which connected much of Europe and parts of Africa by the first century A.D. But even the Romans found it easier to travel by water. Water travel was not only faster, but cheaper. When the Romans traveled by road, they used animals, and animals need to eat a lot of food. Boats don't eat anything!

Ancient Assyrian chariot The Assyrians, who lived in the northern part of present-day Iraq, were great conquerers. Their empire lasted from about 1500 B.C. to 600 B.C.

Peruvian _caballito_ (below)
In modern Peru, coastal fishermen use a raft made of reeds, known as a _caballito_. Their ancestors fished from the same kind of raft more than three thousand years ago.

Arabian _dhow_ off the coast of Kenya Some old ways of making boats are still in use. For example, the Arabian _dhow,_ a sailing ship with triangular sails, was invented in the 1700s. Today, this type of boat is still used in the Red Sea and the Indian Ocean.

more comfortable—and much less bumpy—than riding in a wagon. As for the boat, sails were added to take advantage of the power of the wind.

As you can see, people have worked hard throughout the ages to invent ways to get people and cargo from place to place. One invention led to another. From the cart came the modern car.

Let's take a trip around the world and see how people travel today!

Chinese sculpture, c. 700 A.D. About 4,000 years ago, people in central Asia first tamed the horse and used saddles. About 200 B.C., South Asians invented the stirrup: a footholder attached by straps to the saddle. The stirrup allowed the horse and rider to act as one.

Motor Power

In the 1700s, people began experimenting with ways to make vehicles move all by themselves, without being powered by animals or people. First came the steam engine, which worked because of the pressure created by boiling and then cooling water. Steamboats and steam-driven trains changed the way people thought about distance. Because people could get places faster, everything suddenly seemed much closer.

The problem with steam engines was that it took a lot of coal to keep them running. So, inventors kept looking for additional ways to power vehicles.

Traffic in Bangkok, Thailand
Most motor-powered vehicles run on some kind of fuel. Unfortunately, burning fuel causes air pollution. Pollution from motorized vehicles has become a worldwide problem.

Inventor Henry Ford's first automobile, 1896
By the end of the 1800s, the "horseless carriage" was a reality. Some of the early cars were powered by steam or electricity rather than by gasoline. Today, there are more than 300 million automobiles in the world.

Monorail train, Sydney, Australia

**Motorized wheelchair,
United States**

Solar-powered car, Germany Solar cars are being developed as an alternative to gasoline-powered cars. Because they are powered by energy from the sun rather than by fuel, solar cars are quiet and produce no exhaust. Increase used of such cars could help reduce air pollution and decrease our reliance on fossil fuels.

The electric battery was developed in the 1860s, and the gasoline engine in the 1880s. Together, they made possible the invention of the modern automobile, as well as such vehicles as trucks, motorboats, and airplanes. Today, motor-powered vehicles are used in almost every part of the world. They make it easy to get from one place to another quickly.

Animal Power

Motor-powered vehicles have not taken over the road everywhere. Using animals as transport is still common in many parts of the world. This is especially true in rural areas, where people have held on to traditional ways or can not afford motor-powered vehicles. Besides, animals can get to places that motor-powered vehicles cannot, such as narrow paths on cliffs! Another good thing about animals is that they don't pollute the air.

Amish horse and buggy
The Amish, members of a devout Protestant sect, live in communities in the northeastern and midwestern United States. Their religious beliefs forbid the use of motor-powered vehicles.

Costa Rica "singing" cart Oxen are used as draft animals (animals that pull loads) in countries all over the world. Costa Rica is famous for its traditional "singing" oxcarts. These colorful vehicles get their name from the noise the wheels make as they move along. The designs painted on the carts vary from region to region.

Water buffalo, Malaysia
Water buffaloes, which can wade through dense swamps without difficulty, are commonly used as work animals in swampy areas of Malaysia, Indonesia, and the Philippines.

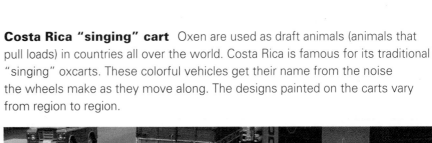

Dogsled in the Yukon Territory, Canada Sleds pulled by huskies are an important means of transportation in parts of Alaska and northern Canada, where snow covers the ground much of the year.

Mule, Morocco A mule is a cross between a horse and a donkey. Mules are often used as pack animals in Mediterranean countries.

Bororo nomads loading a donkey, Niger Donkeys, though smaller than horses, are strong and sturdy. They are often used as pack animals in mountainous or desert areas that lack modern roads.

People Power

Even with the availability of motors and animals, people have not completely given up the most basic way of getting vehicles to move: using their own muscles! Everywhere you go, you'll find human-powered vehicles, from bicycle to rowboats to baby strollers!

Madagascar *pousse-pousse* In Antananarivo, the capital of Madagascar, the *pousse-pousse* is used only for transporting packages. Outside the capital, the *pousse-pousse* is still used to carry people. It gets its name from the French word *"pousse,"* which means "push." Madagascar was once a French colony.

The "Boneshaker" The pedaled bicycle was invented in the early 1800s. At first, it was a very awkward vehicle, with wooden wheels and pedals that were hard to operate. But by tinkering with its design, people gradually made improvements. The most important development came in 1888, when Irish inventor John Boyd Dunlop perfected air-filled rubber tires. Until then, riding a bicycle was a very bumpy experience! In fact, a popular French bicycle of the 1860s was nicknamed the "boneshaker"!

Becap, Java, Indonesia In many parts of Asia, pedicabs are a popular means of transportation. A pedicab is like a bicycle, but it has three wheels and has a passenger carriage at the front or rear. In Java, pedicabs are called *becaps*.

Hand-operated cable-car bridge, Peru

Madeira *carro*, 1920s Traditionally, people traveled down the steep hills of the Portuguese island of Madeira on a *carro*—a sledge. A driver steered the *carro*, with its passengers, down the hill and then carried the empty *carro* all the way back up. *Carros* are still in use today—but only for tourists!

By Land or By Sea?

The kind of vehicle that people use depends partly on their environment. In hot, dry, desert areas, for example, camels are great vehicles. They can store large amounts of food and water in their bodies, and so they can go days without "fuel." Camels also walk easily on soft sand and can carry up to six hundred pounds of passengers and goods. Today, camels are used for desert travel in many parts of Africa and Asia.

Reindeer sled, Lapland Animal-drawn sleds are still used by many native Arctic people, especially in Lapland, where the Sami people have chosen to maintain a traditional way of life. Lapland is a region in far northern Europe, above the arctic circle.

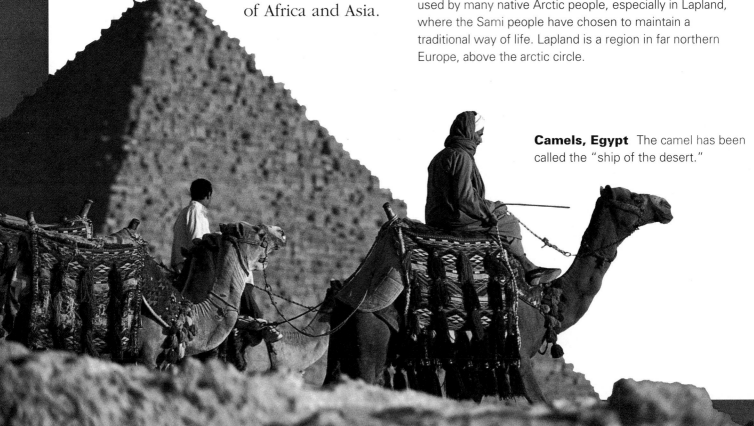

Camels, Egypt The camel has been called the "ship of the desert."

Llamas The llama is sure-footed, can maintain a steady pace for hours, and can go without food and water for long periods of time. It is used as a pack animal in the Andes Mountains of South America.

Different forms of transportation are needed in cold, snowy environments. In the Arctic, for example, the traditional vehicle was a sled pulled by dogs or reindeer. Today, the people of the Arctic tend to use snowmobiles on land and speedboats in the water, although animal-drawn sleds are still popular in some places.

For travel in mountainous countries, people often use strong animals that can stand the high altitude and the cold (which horses, for example, cannot). Peruvians have long used llamas to carry goods in the Andes Mountains.

Yak, Tibet The yak, an Asian type of ox, is the main form of transportation in the incredibly high Himalaya mountains of Tibet. Yaks are strong, agile animals that can withstand Tibet's altitude and cold, dry climate. They are able to carry heavy loads 20 miles a day.

In Tibet, a region of China, and in the nearby country of Nepal, people still use their traditional mountain vehicle: the shaggy-haired yak. The mountains of Tibet and Nepal are the highest in the world.

People who live in watery environments have their own special ways of traveling. In Venice, an Italian city that was built on a group of islands, people either walk along the narrow streets and bridges or ride boats along the canals. Venice is perhaps the quietest city in Italy because there are no cars. About all you hear are footsteps and the swish of poles and paddles in the water! In the Asian countries of Laos and Bangladesh, people also rely on boats for most of their travel. This is because a good system of roads has not been developed. Traveling along the rivers is the fastest and easiest way to get around.

Coastal village, Benin The coastal area of the African country of Benin is made up of tidal marshes and lagoons. People who live in this region travel mainly by boat.

Elevated cable car, Norway

A modern way to travel up a mountain is to take an elevated cable car, a vehicle that runs on wire cables suspended between towers.

Gondolas, Venice, Italy Traditionally, people traveled around Venice in long boats called gondolas. Today, gondolas are used mainly by tourists. Many residents of the city have their own rowboats.

Lunar rover

This vehicle was designed for a very special environment: the moon!

Across Town . . . or Across the Miles?

The kind of vehicle that people use also depends on how far they are going. There are vehicles for short distances . . .

Heua hang yao boat, Laos A long-tailed boat, or *heua hang yao*, is used for short trips in Laos. Large diesel-engine ferries are usually used for long distances in Laos.

Tonga, Pakistan In Pakistan, India, and parts of Myanmar, people use *tongas*—horse-drawn carts— to go short distances.

Bicycles in Shanghai, China, and Bruges, Belgium In many countries, the bicycle is the most popular way to get around. People ride bicycles to work, to school—anywhere that's not too far! In the Netherlands, where nearly everyone owns a bike, there are almost as many bike paths as streets! Bicycles are very popular in Belgium, too. And in many Chinese cities, bicycles rule the road. Bicycle-riding doesn't pollute the air or add much to the crowding of city streets— and it's a great way to stay in shape!

Mopeds in Athens, Greece
Lightweight motorbikes called mopeds are used for traveling short distances in many countries, especially in crowded urban areas that have narrow streets. People in many southern European cities, like Athens and Rome, use mopeds to dash in and out of automobile traffic.

. . . and vehicles for long distances!

It used to be that most people lived their whole lives without ever leaving their hometown, let alone visiting another country. Today, more of us travel far from home—for work and for pleasure—than ever before. Modern transportation has made the world seem much smaller. We're now only a hop, a skip, and a jump from anywhere we want to go!

Ocean-going passenger ship, New York

High-speed "Bullet" train, Japan In Japan and many European countries, people can travel between cities on high-speed electric trains. The Japanese "Bullet" train reaches speeds of 160 miles per hour!

Space shuttle Long-distance travel has come a long way; we can now travel thousands of miles into space. We can even travel to the moon!

Passenger airplane, Venezuela
Orville and Wilbur Wright developed the first motor-powered airplane in 1903. At that time, people could travel across the ocean only by ship. Today, planes are commonly used for long-distance travel. The increased use of airplanes has led to a decrease in travel on huge passenger ships.

Traveling in Style

Another thing that affects the kind of vehicle that people use is how much money they can afford to spend. Some vehicles cost more to buy and operate than others. Expensive vehicles are usually more comfortable than less expensive ones. They are also more prestigious; they make the owner look good in the eyes of other people in his or her society.

Throughout history, rich and powerful people have used expensive means of transportation to display their wealth and high status in society. In India, for example, members of the royal family once traveled by elephant. Not only did elephants cost a lot of money, but being on top of an elephant makes a person seem more important than all those other people down on the ground! Today, a wealthy bride and groom in India may travel to their wedding by elephant. In Korea, it was once the fashion for wealthy women to travel in a *ga-ma*, a kind of carriage that was carried by four servants.

Italian Ferrari Sometimes, a car says something about how its owner wants to be viewed by others. The owner of a sleek, sporty Ferrari, for example, may want to be seen as wealthy, dashing, and adventurous.

Korean *ga-ma*

British Concorde The fastest, most luxurious, and most expensive way to travel is aboard the Concorde, an SST (supersonic transport). Built by Great Britain and France, it travels at speeds of 1,550 miles per hour, and can fly from Paris to New York in under four hours!

Indian elephant Traditionally, traveling by elephant was a sign of high status in Indian society.

Today, the *ga-ma* is still used in traditional Korean weddings.

But what is prestigious in one culture, or one period in history, may not be prestigious in another. Three thousand years ago, riding in a wagon pulled by oxen was a sign of high status in central and southeastern Europe. Some people even chose to be buried with their wagon!

Public Transportation

In terms of travel, the difference between rich people and poor people was much greater in the past than it is today. In the past, rich people could travel, while most poor people couldn't. Up until a couple hundred years ago, if you weren't rich enough to own a horse and carriage—and few people were—you had to walk to where you wanted to go.

That changed dramatically in the 1800s. What happened? Public transportation! In 1812, the omnibus was invented in France. It was a horse-drawn vehicle that could carry lots of passengers. The word "omnibus" comes from a Latin word meaning "for all." People could afford to ride the omnibus because they all shared the cost of the ride. You didn't need to buy your own horse and carriage if you could "buy" a ride on someone else's!

Today, public transportation is available in some form in most parts of the world, but the exact type varies from place to place. Buses are a very common form of mass transportation. They usually take a fixed route, with passengers getting on and off at designated stops.

Double-decker bus, Hong Kong
Buses in Hong Kong that have two levels for passengers are called "double-deckers." London is another city famous for its double-decker buses.

Buses in Accra, Ghana In developing countries, which sometimes cannot afford to buy new buses, used vehicles—such as pickup trucks—are often converted into buses.

Jeepney, Philippines *Jeepneys* are colorful minibuses built on the frames of old military jeeps. They travel on relatively fixed routes, and stop when waved at from the sidewalk. On the outside, *jeepneys* are painted all kinds of colors. On the inside, they may be decorated with fun things like mirrored balls, stickers, lights, and tassels!

New Zealand bus

Haitian *tap-tap* The *tap-tap,* a brightly painted converted pickup truck, is the main form of public transportation in Haiti. Its name comes from the sound made by its diesel engine.

Automobile taxi, Argentina

Taxis are also common throughout the world. A taxi is a vehicle for hire; it often carries only one passenger at a time and usually picks up the passenger where he or she is and goes only where that passenger wants to go. Some Asian and African countries have taxis that are used a little more like buses. They are

***Tuk-tuk*, Thailand** The *tuk-tuk* is a type of motorized three-wheeled taxi used in Thai cities.

Automobile taxi, British Columbia, Canada This taxi is specially designed to accommodate passengers who use wheelchairs.

Truck taxi, Niger In Niger, trucks are often used to transport both passengers and goods over long distances. As many passengers as possible perch on top of the cargo, which is usually sacks of grain or fertilizer.

station wagons or trucks that can carry six or more people. However, unlike a bus, this kind of taxi doesn't go anywhere until there are enough passengers aboard, and its route isn't fixed.

Motorcycle taxi, Cambodia

In some countries, the cheapest and most efficient form of long-distance transportation is the train. Almost every country has at least one railroad. In industrialized countries, diesel-electric locomotives are the most widely used trains. In many developing countries of Africa, Asia, and South America, steam locomotives are still widely used.

Electric streetcars in Budapest, Hungary
The electric streetcar, or tram, is a form of public transportation found in many cities. It is a vehicle that runs on rails along city streets. The first streetcar was invented in 1832. It was pulled by horses! Electric streetcars were invented in 1879 in Berlin, Germany.

Intercity train, Switzerland
The train is a wonderful way to travel in many countries. You can sit back and enjoy the countryside!

San Francisco cable car Not all streetcars are electric. Some—like those in San Francisco—are pulled by an underground cable powered by a regular engine at a central station.

Moscow Metro The subway was invented for city travel. Because it is underground, it doesn't add to crowding and noise on city streets. The first subway opened in 1863 in London, England. Today, subways are found in cities all over the world. The people of Moscow, Russia, are proud of their subway system. It has the world's fanciest subway stations, and each has a different design.

Many of the world's cities have their own electric railway systems to help people get around within the city. These trains are powered by electricity from an overhead power line or an electrified third rail. They may run underground (subways), above the ground (elevated trains), or in the street (streetcars or trams). Electric railways are faster and quieter than regular trains and do not pollute. They help keep city air clean!

Vehicles for Every Need

As you can see, people use a variety of vehicles to go places, whether it's to school, across town, or to grandmother's house across the country.

People use other kinds of vehicles to transport goods across land, across water, and through the air. Trucks, barges and ocean freighters, and cargo planes are a few examples.

People also use vehicles to perform special tasks, like putting out fires or plowing fields. Fire trucks and tractors are special-purpose vehicles, as are helicopters, ambulances, tanks, and other military vehicles.

Helicopter, Ontario, Canada The helicopter is an aircraft that is lifted off the ground by one or more rotors, or spinning blades. Because helicopters don't need runways, can travel in any direction, and can even hover, they can take off and land in areas too small for airplanes. This makes them excellent vehicles for such special purposes as emergency rescue and traffic observation.

Tuareg salt caravan A nomadic people called the Tuareg, who live in the Saharan desert in northern Africa, use camel caravans to transport salt.

Floating market, Thailand

Harvesting wheat with a combine, United States

Fire truck, Chile

And of course, people use some vehicles just for fun!

Bumper car, United States

Glossary

accommodate make suitable for (p.26)

alternative something one can choose instead of another thing (p.9)

altitude height above sea level (p.16)

appreciate to be aware of the worth of (p.4)

axle a bar on which wheels turn (p.5)

barge a large, flat-bottomed boat used to carry freight in inland waters (p.30)

canal a waterway built by humans and used for travel, irrigation, or shipping (p.16)

cargo freight carried by ship, aircraft, truck, or train (p.7)

civilization a complex society with a stable food supply, division of labor, some form of government, and a highly developed culture (p.5)

colony a territory governed by a distant country (p.13)

culture the beliefs and customs of a group of people that are passed from one generation to another (p.23)

devout religious (p.10)

diesel engine an internal combustion engine that works by injecting burning oil into hot compressed air (p.18)

diesel-electric locomotive a locomotive powered by a diesel engine driving an electric generator (p.28)

environment a person's natural surroundings (p.14)

exhaust the waste gases or fumes that escape from an engine (p.9)

fossil fuel a type of fuel—like oil, coal, or natural gas—that is formed in the earth from ancient plant and animal remains (p.9)

marsh an area of low, wet land (p.5)

pack animal an animal used to carry goods or people on its back (p.11)

reliance dependence (p.9)

rural located in the country (p.10)

status the position or rank of a person in relation to others in his or her society (p.22)

traditional handed down from generation to generation (p.10)

transportation the means by which people or goods are moved from one place to another (p.4)

urban located in a city (p.19)

Index

About the Author

Karin Luisa Badt has a Ph.D. in comparative literature from the University of Chicago and a B.A. in literature and society from Brown University. She likes to travel and live in foreign countries. Ms. Badt has taught at the University of Rome and the University of Chicago.